VOICE CONTROLLED WIRELESS ELECTRONIC NOTICE BOARD USING ANDROID

GOKULALAKSHMI S

Contents

SYNOPSIS

Voice commands are used to change scrolling message on Electronic Notice Board. Bluetooth is used as wireless communication technique. Android app does the function of speech recognition. Main concept behind Voice operated Electronic notice board using rolling display is to show scrolling messages and to control them by using our own voice. We have already seen GSM based Electronic Notice board, however speech controlled Notice board has additional advantage of ease of use. User has to give voice command in his/her own voice to control the scrolling messages displayed on electronic notice board. Voice recognition is done in the Android application. User has to install this Android application in his/her smart phone or tablet. Then user has to give voice commands to this android app. Android app then passes these commands to the microcontroller using wireless communication. It means user doesn't have to go near the Electronic notice board to change the scrolling message. Microcontroller receives these commands with the help of Bluetooth receiver and decoder. Then it passes these commands to the Rolling display which is made up of the LED Display.

CHAPTER ONE

INTRODUCTION

The project is an electronic notice board that is controlled by an android device and displays message on it. Traditionally, there were notice boards where any information or notice had to be stick daily. This becomes tedious and requires daily maintenance.

The project overcomes this problem by introducing an electronic display notice board interfaced to an android device through Bluetooth connectivity. The Bluetooth receives the message from the android device that is sent to a microcontroller. The microcontroller displays the message on a LCD screen. This project can be used in colleges, offices, railway stations or airports for displaying any information.

The main objective of the project is to develop a wireless notice board that displays notices when a message is sent from the user's android application device. Remote operation is achieved by any smart- phone/Tablet etc., with Android OS, upon a GUI (Graphical User Interface) based touch screen operation. While the user sends the message from the android application device, it is received and retrieved by the Bluetooth device at the display unit. It is then sent to the microcontroller that further displays the notice sent from the user on to the electronic notice board which is equipped with a LED display

CHAPTER TWO

BLOCK DIAGRAM

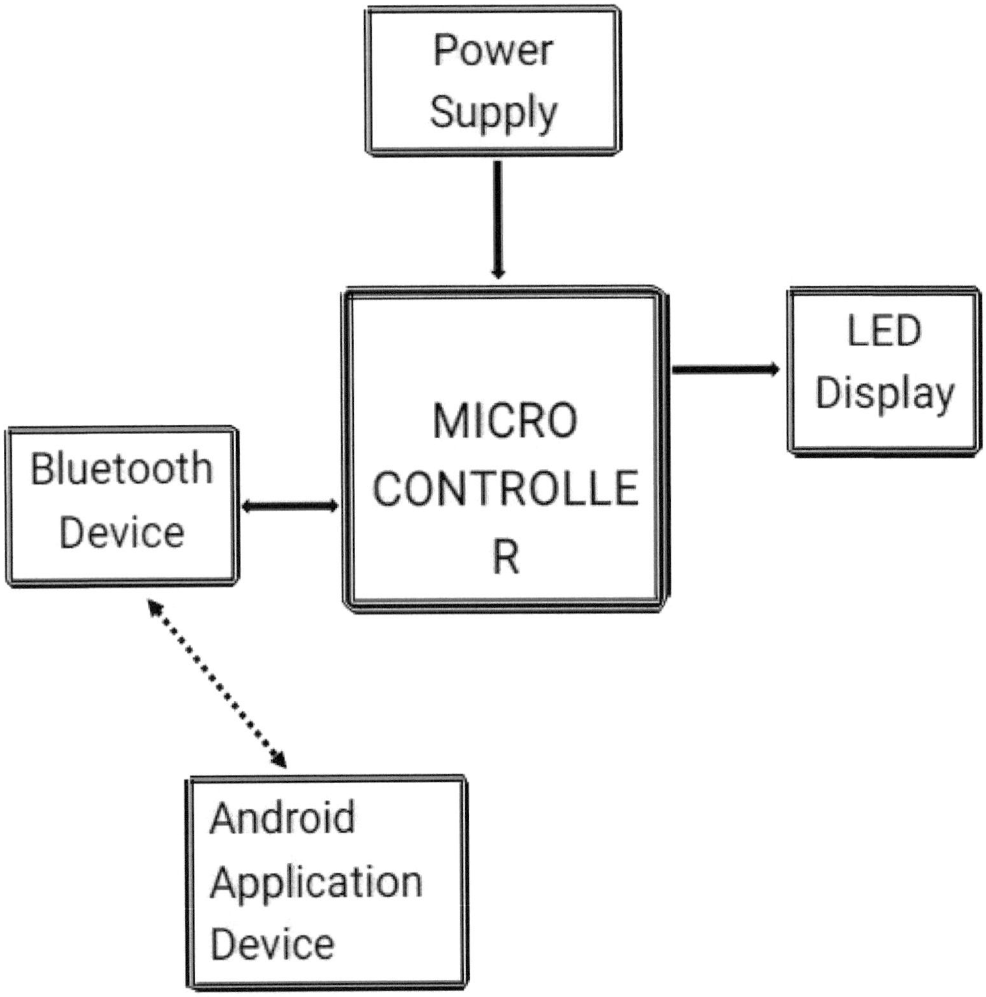

BLOCK DIAGRAM DESCRIPTION

This project consists of MAX232, Atmega328 controller, LED module for display and Bluetooth serial module for communication. Power supply is used to supply the all units. It is used to convert AC to constant DC voltage. In this project we use atmega328 controller. ATMEGA 328 microcontroller, which acts as a processor for the arduino board. Nearly it consists of 28 pins. From these 28 pins, the inputs can be controlled by transmitting and receiving the inputs to the external device. Bluetooth module HC05 is connected to controller through interfacing unit. MAX232 is used as interfacing unit. It is used for serial communication between controller and Bluetooth module. The information is transmitted using an android phone. Controller to display the information in LED display. Driver is used to drive the scrolling LED display. Whenever user send the message on Electronic Notice board, then user has to type a message on an application installed on Android mobile and send it to the microcontroller using Bluetooth technology.

CHAPTER THREE

CIRCUIT DIAGRAM

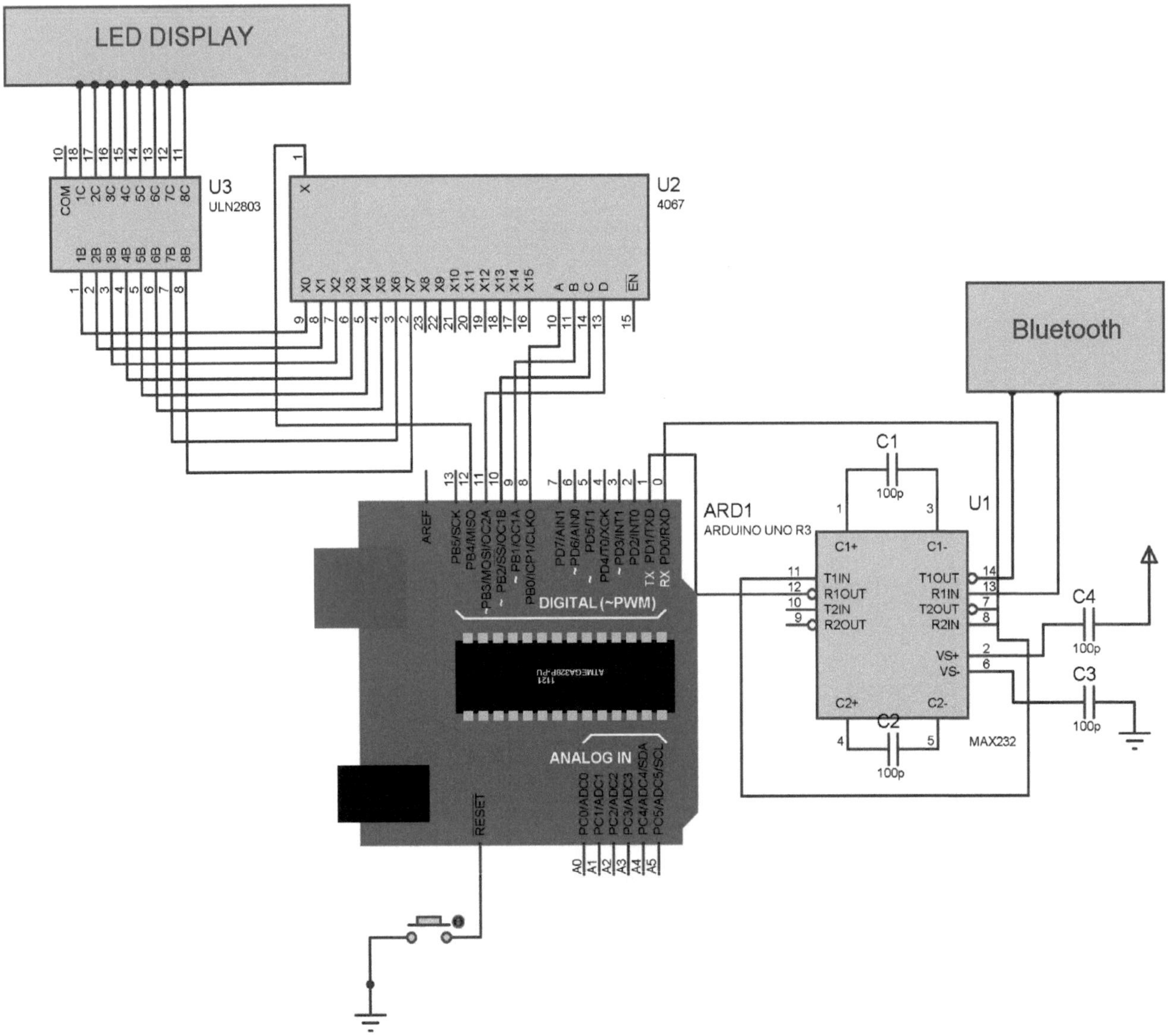

CIRCUIT DESCRIPTION

In this project we use atmega328 controller, it has 28 ports. Reset switch is connected to controller port 1 for resetting purpose. In this system to design a LED based scrolling message display control from an android mobile phone. This system makes the use of Bluetooth technology to communicate from android phone to LED Display board. Bluetooth module HC05 is connected to max232 port 13 & 14. MAX is connected to controller port 0 & 1. It is used for serial communication between controller and Bluetooth module. Controller receive the signal from android mobile via Bluetooth. Controller to run the LED display through driver. Controller signal is given to multiplexer IC4067. Multiplexer input port A, B, C & D is connected to controller port 8, 9, 10 & 11. Multiplexer data is given to LED driver (ULN2803) unit. Multiplexer data X0 to X8 is connected to driver input port 1 to 8. Driver output ports are connected to LED display.

CHAPTER FOUR

HARDWARE DETAILS

SINGLE POWER SUPPLY:

Power supply gives supply to all components. It is used to convert AC voltage into DC voltage. Transformer used to convert 230V into 12V AC.12V AC is given to diode. Diode range is 1N4007, which is used to convert AC voltage into DC voltage. AC capacitor used to charge AC components and discharge on ground. LM 7805 regulator is used to maintain voltage as constant. Then signal will be given to next capacitor, which is used to filter unwanted AC component. Load will be LED and resister. LED voltage is 1.75V.if voltage is above level beyond the limit, and then it will be dropped on resister.

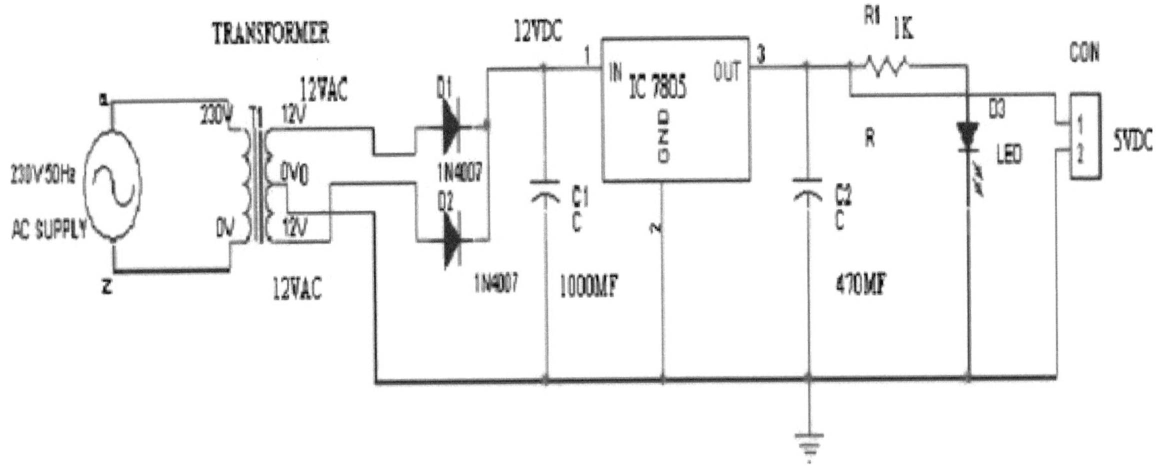

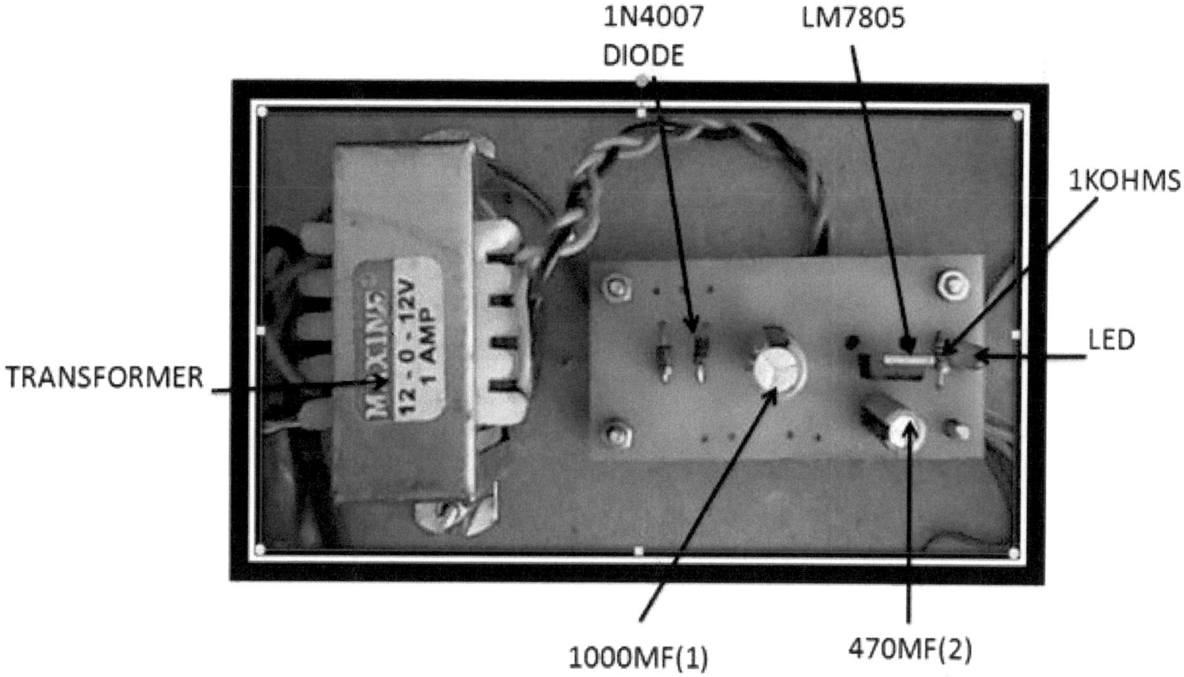

POWER SUPPLY

Most electronic circuits require DC voltage sources or power supplies. If the electronic device is to be portable, then one or more batteries are usually needed to provide the DC voltage required by electronic circuits. But batteries have a limited life span and cannot be recharged. The solution is to convert the alternating current lose hold line voltage to a DC voltage source.

BLOCK DIAGRAM FOR POWER SUPPLY

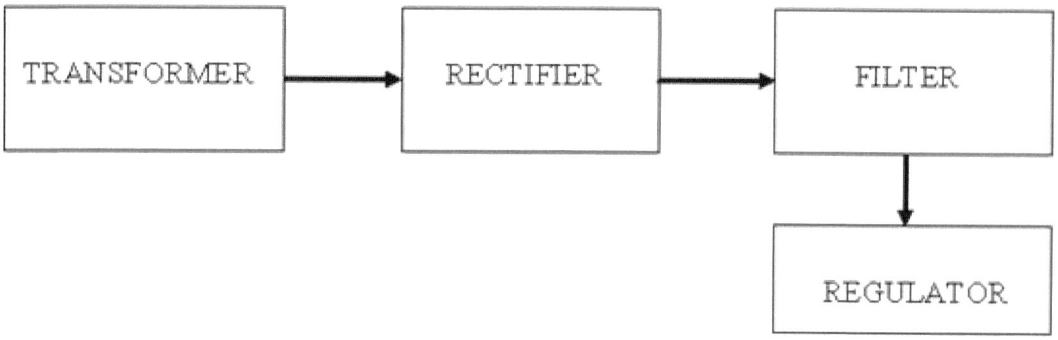

Block diagram of AC to DC power Supply consists,

1. *Transformer: Steps the household line voltage up or downas required.*
2. *Rectifier: Converts ac voltage into dc voltage.*
3. *Filter: Smooth the pulsating DC voltage to a varying DC voltage.*
4. *Regulator: Fix the output voltage to constant value.*

Brief Introduction to an Electrical Transformer

A Transformer is an electrical device that takes electricity of one voltage and changes it into another voltage. In AC circuits, AC voltage, current and waveform can be transformed with the help of Transformers. Transformer plays an important role in electronic equipment. AC and DC voltage in Power supply equipment are almost achieved by transformer's transformation and commutation. Figure 1 shows the Transformer.

Basically, a Transformer changes electricity from high to low voltage or low to high voltage using two properties of electricity. In an electric circuit, there is magnetism around it. Second, whenever a magnetic field changes (by moving or by changing strength) a voltage is made.

A Transformer takes in electricity at a higher voltage and lets it run through lots of coils wound around an iron core. ". A single-phase

Transformer can operate to either increase or decrease the voltage applied to the primary winding. Because the current is alternating, the magnetism in the core is also alternating. Also around the core is an output wire with fewer coils. The magnetism changing back and forth makes a current in the wire. Having fewer coils means less voltage. When it is used to "decrease" the voltage on the secondary winding with respect to the primary it is called a ***Step-down Transformer****. When a Transformer is used to "increase" the voltage on its secondary winding with respect to the primary, it is called a* ***Step-up Transformer****.*

However, a third condition exists in which a transformer produces the same voltage on its secondary as is applied to its primary winding. In other words, its output is identical with respect to input. This type of Transformer is called an ***"Impedance Transformer"*** *and is mainly used for impedance matching or the isolation of adjoining electrical circuits.*

Working of a Transformer

The working principle of Transformer is very simple. It depends upon Faraday's law of electromagnetic induction. Actually, mutual induction between two or more winding is responsible for transformation action in an Electrical Transformer.

According to Faraday's laws of electromagnetic

induction,

"Rate of change of flux linkage with respect to time is directly proportional to the induced EMF in a conductor or coil".

When one winding which is supplied by an alternating electrical source as shown in figure 2. The alternating current through the winding produces a continually changing flux or alternating flux that surrounds the winding. If any other winding is brought nearer to the previous one, obviously some portion of this flux will link with the second. As this flux is continually changing in its amplitude and direction, there must be a change in flux linkage in the second winding or coil.

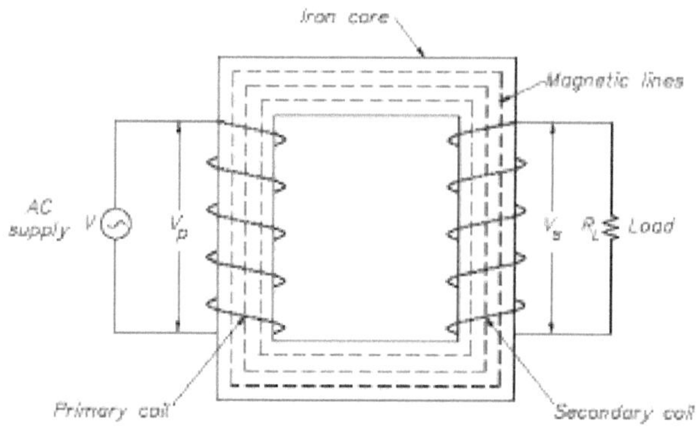

According to Faraday's law, there must be an EMF induced in the second. If the circuit of the later winding is closed, there must be an electric current flowing through it.

Now let us see the working of a Transformer in detail. The winding which takes electrical power from the source, is generally known as Primary winding of Transformer as shown in figure

1. *The winding which gives the desired output voltage due to mutual induction in the transformer, is commonly known as Secondary winding of Transformer.*

The difference in voltage between the Primary and the Secondary windings is achieved by changing the number of coil turns in the Primary winding compared to the number of coil turns on the Secondary winding.

As the Transformer is a linear device, a ratio is done between the numbers of turns of the primary coil divided by the number of turns of the secondary coil. This ratio, called the ratio of transformation, more commonly known as a Transformers "turns ratio". This turn's ratio value dictates the operation of the Transformer and the corresponding voltage available on the secondary winding.

If the Transformer's ratio is 10:1, then if there are 2200 volts on the Primary winding there will be 220 volts on the Secondary winding. Then we can see that if the ratio between the numbers of turns changes the resulting voltages must also change by the same ratio.

Rectifiers

A rectifier circuit converts an AC voltage into a pulsating DC voltage. This is accomplished by using one or more diodes because diodes conduct current in only one direction.

Types of Rectifiers:

- *Half-wave Rectifier*
- *Full-wave Rectifier*
- *Full-wave bridge rectifier*

Full-wave bridge rectifier:

The full-wave bridge rectifier circuit requires four diodes. The transformer has only one secondary winding.

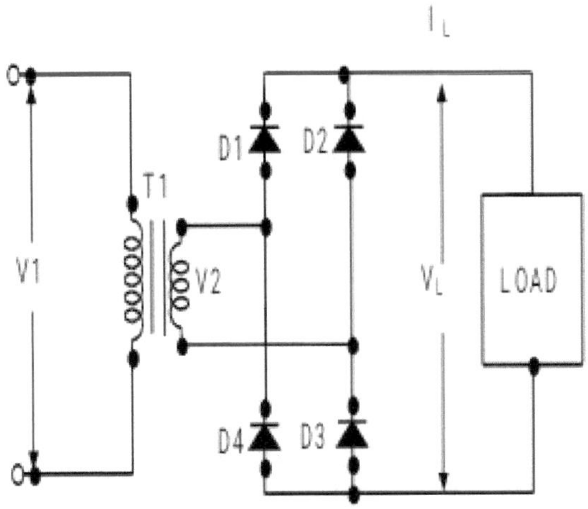

When V2 is positive, diodes D1 & D3 conduct current through the load. Diodes D2 and D4 block current flow. When V2 is negative, diodes D2 and D4 conduct current through the load. Diodes D1 and D3 block current flow. The full-wave bridge rectifier fully utilizes the transformer winding during both half cycles.

USEFUL FORMULAS

VL (DC) = 0.637V2

VL (AC) = 0.307V2

%RIPPLE = VL (AC)/VL (DC) = 48.2%

RIPPLE FREQUENCY = 2 x SUPPLY FREQUENCY

Filters:

The 121% ripple in the output of the half-wave rectifier and 48% in the full-wave rectifier is more than can be normally tolerated. In the full wave filtering, wherein the frequency of the ripple is 100Hz for a 50Hz ac line voltage. This is an advantage where either an inductor is used to prevent the passage of the ripple current(due to its high inductive reactance to ac but quite low resistance to dc), or a capacitor is used to 'short' the ripple to ground but leave the dc to appear at the output. Various combinations of L and C are also used.

Regulators:

The simplest regulator is a large capacitor in parallel with the load. The capacitor stores DC voltage while the load voltage increases to its peak value. The capacitor converts the pulsating DC voltage of a rectifier into a smooth Dc load voltage.

Two important parameters of a capacitor regulator are its working voltage and its capacitance. The working voltage must be at least equal to no-load output voltage of power supply. The capacitance determines the amount of ripple that appears on the Dc output when current is drawn from the circuit. The amount of ripple decreases with increase in capacitance.

PIN DETAILS:

IC 7805:

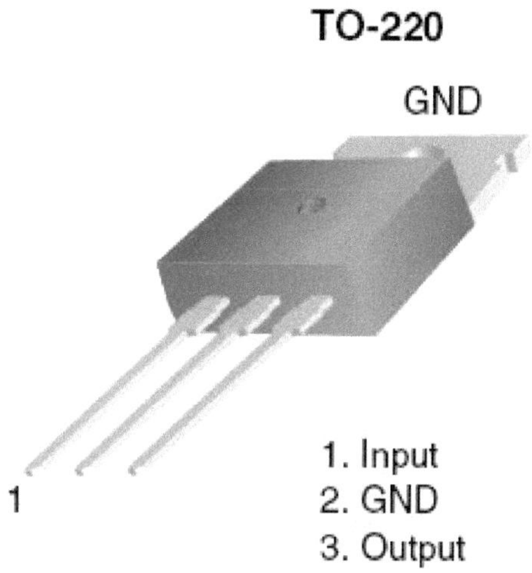

FEATURES:
1.Suitable for TTL, DTL, HTL, C-MOS Power supply.
2.Internal short-circuit current limiting.
3.Internal Thermal Overload Protection.
4.Maximum Output Current of 150mA.
5.Packaged in TO-92.
Electrical characteristics:
Input voltage : 5V~15V.
Power dissipation : 600mW.
Operating Junction Temperature :-30~150 °C.
Operating Temperature :-30~75 °C.
CAPACITORS:

Features:

** Enabled high ripple current by a reduction of impedance at high frequency range.*

** Load*

** Life 105°C 2000~5000hours.*

** Operating Temperature Range :-40~+105°C.*

** Rated Voltage Range :6.3~100V.*

** Capacitance Tolerance :±20%(20°C,120Hz).*

Resistor:

Resistor Color Code:

An electronic color code is a code that is used to specify the ratings of certain electrical components, such as the resistance in Ohms of a resistor. Electronic color codes are also used to rate capacitors, inductors, diodes, and other electronic components, but are most typically used for resistors. Only resistors are addressed by this calculator.

How the color coding works:

The color coding for resistors is an international standard that is defined in IEC 60062. The resistor color code shown in the table below involves various colors that represent significant figures, multiplier, tolerance, reliability, and temperature coefficient. Which of these the color refers to is dependent on the position of the color band on the resistor. In a typical four-band resistor, there is a spacing between the third and the fourth band to indicate how the resistor should be read (from left to right, with the lone band after the spacing being the right-most band). In the explanation below, a four-band resistor (the one specifically shown below) will be used. Other possible resistor variations will be described after.

Significant figure component:

In a typical four-band resistor, the first and second bands represent significant figures. For this example, refer to the figure above with a green, red, blue, and gold band. Using the table provided below, the green band represents the number 5, and the red band is 2.

Multiplier:

The third, blue band, is the multiplier. Using the table, the multiplier is thus 1,000,000. This multiplier is multiplied by the significant figures determined from the previous bands, in this case 52, resulting in a value of 52,000,000 Ω, or 52 MΩ.

Tolerance:

The fourth band is not always present, but when it is, represents tolerance. This is a percentage by which the resistor value can vary. The gold band in this example indicates a tolerance of ±5%, which can be represented by the letter J. This means that the value 52 MΩ can vary by up to 5% in either direction, so the value of the resistor is 49.4 MΩ - 54.6 MΩ.

Reliability, temperature coefficient, and other variations:

Coded components have at least three bands: two significant figure bands and a multiplier, but there are other possible variations. For example, components that are made to military specifications are typically four-band resistors that may have a fifth band that indicates the reliability of the resistor in terms of failure rate percentage per 1000 hours of service. It is also possible to have a 5th band that is the temperature coefficient, which indicates the change in resistance of the component as a function of ambient temperature in terms of ppm/K.

More commonly, there are five-band resistors that are more precise due to a third significant figure band. This shifts the position of the multiplier and tolerance band into the 4th and 5th position as compared to a typical four-band resistor.

On the most precise of resistors, a 6th band may be present. The first three bands would be the significant figure bands, the 4th the multiplier, the 5th the tolerance, and the 6th could be either reliability or temperature coefficient. There are also other possible variations, but these are some of the more common configurations.

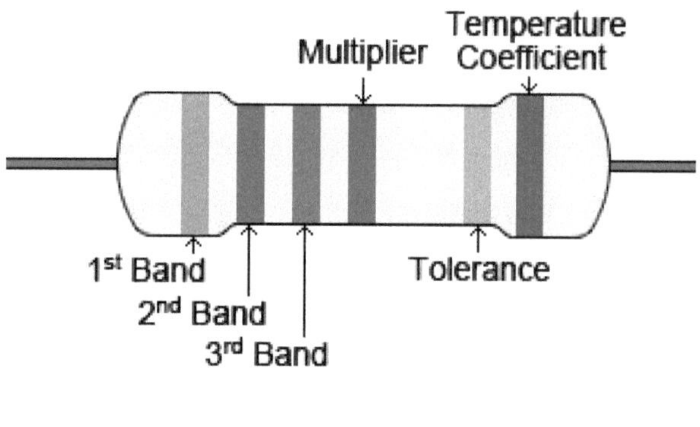

Black	0	0	$\times 10^0$		
Brown	1	1	$\times 10^1$	±1% (F)	100 ppm
Red	2	2	$\times 10^2$	±2% (G)	50 ppm
Orange	3	3	$\times 10^3$		15 ppm
Yellow	4	4	$\times 10^4$		25 ppm
Green	5	5	$\times 10^5$	±0.5% (D)	
Blue	6	6	$\times 10^6$	±0.25% (C)	
Violet	7	7	$\times 10^7$	±0.1% (B)	
Gray	8	8	$\times 10^8$	±0.05% (A)	
White	9	9	$\times 10^9$		
Gold			$\times 10^{-1}$	±5% (J)	
Silver			$\times 10^{-2}$	±10% (K)	
None				±20% (M)	

Features:

** Temperature Range -55°C ~ +155°C*

** ±5% tolerance*

** High quality performance at economical prices*

** Compatible with automatic insertion equipment*

** Flame retardant type available*

** Tin coated annealed copper wire.*

CHAPTER FIVE

LIGHT EMITTIND DIODE (LED)

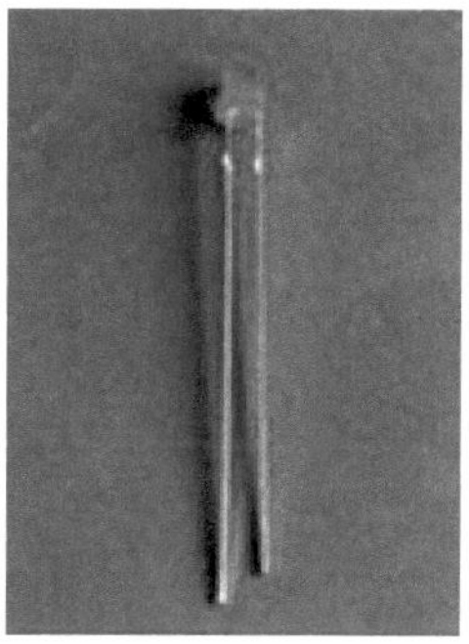

Enter Caption

Features:

** Choice of various viewing angles*

** Available on tape and reel.*

** Reliable and robust*

** Consumes very power.*

Electrical characteristics:

1.*Forward Current* (IF):15 mA

2.*Operating Temperature (Topr): -40 to +85 ℃*

3.*Storage Temperature (Tstg) 40 to +100 ℃*

4.*Soldering Temperature(Tsol) 260 ± 5 ℃*

5.*Power Dissipation (Pd) : 45 mW*

6.*Peak Forward Current (IF Peak) 50 mA*

7.*Reverse Voltage(VR) :5 V*

CHAPTER SIX

ATMEGA 328

ATMEGA 328 microcontroller, which acts as a processor for the arduino board. Nearly it consists of 28 pins. From these 28 pins, the inputs can be controlled by transmitting and receiving the inputs to the external device. It also consists of pulse width modulation (PWM). These PWM are used to transmit the entire signal in a pulse modulation. Input power supply such as Vcc and Gnd are used. These IC mainly consists of analog and digital inputs. These analog and digital inputs are used for the process of certain applications.

CHAPTER SEVEN

DESCRIPTION OF INPUT

ANALOG INPUT:

Arduino atmega-328 microcontroller board consist of 6 analog inputs pins. These analog inputs can be named from A0 to A5. From these 6 analog inputs pins, we can do the process by using analog inputs. Analog inputs can be used in the operating range of 0 to 5V. Analog signal is considered as the continuous time signal, from which these analog signal can be used for certain applications. These are also called as non discrete time signal. Inputs such as voltage, current etc.., are considered to be either analog signal or digital signal only by analysing the time signal properties. Various applications of arduino microcontroller can use only an analog input instead of digital inputs. For these applications, analog input ports or pins can be used.

DIGITAL INPUT:

Digital inputs can be defined as the non continuous time signal with discrete input pulses. It can be represented as 0's and 1's. These digital inputs can be either on state or in off state. Arduino atmega328 microcontroller also consists of 12 digital input pins. It can be stated as D0 to D11. Nearly 12 inputs can be used for digital input/output applications. The working of the digital input ports is where the discrete input pulses can be triggered and supplied to the ports. These ports receive the input and therefore the port can be used for both input and output process. These digital pins can access only the digital inputs.

ATMEGA-328 IC:

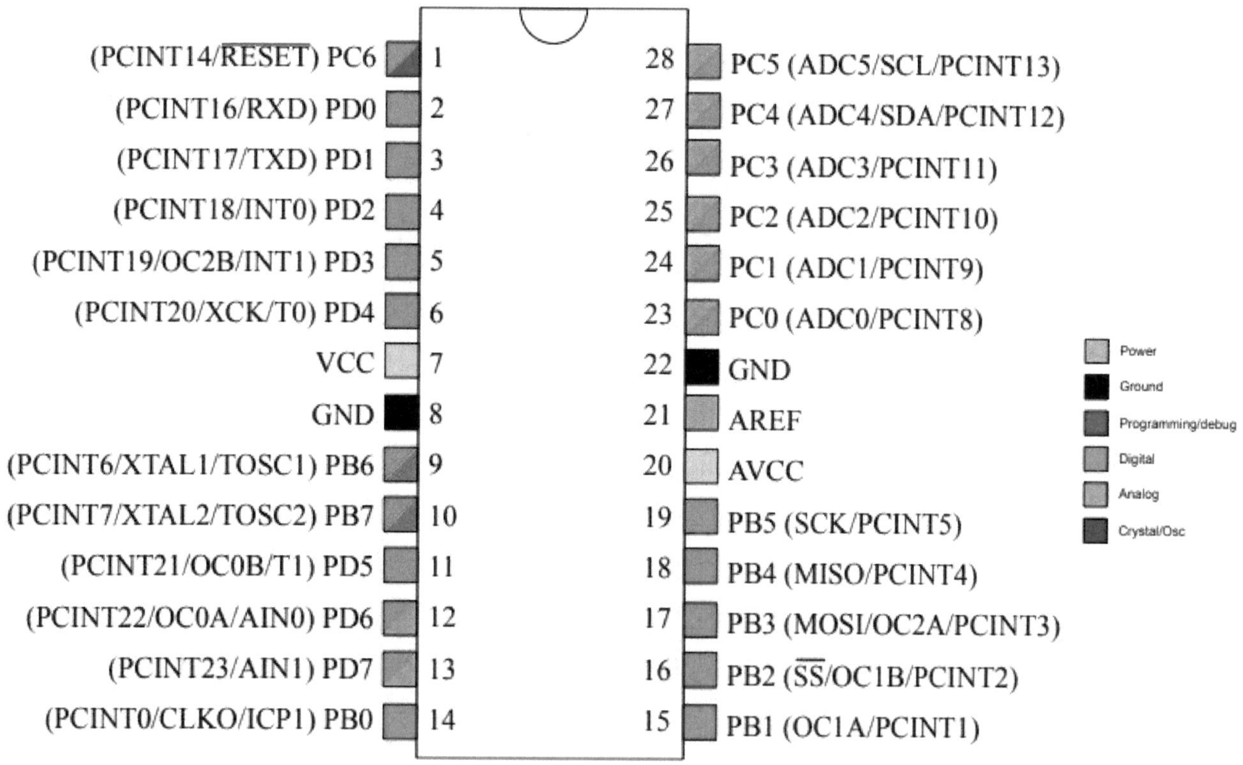

This ATMEGA-328 integrated chip consists of 28 pins. It consists of 6 analog inputs that are shown in the pin diagram. Analog inputs can be represented as PC0 to PC5. These analog input pins possess the continuous time signal which acts as an analog input for the system. Further it also consists of 12 digital inputs. It can be represented as PD1 to PD11 which act as a digital input ports based on pulse width modulation (PWM). These PWM, which transmits the signal in the form of discredited form. Both analog and digital input ports can be used for various applications for the input power supply, VCC and GND pins are used. Pins PB6 and PB7, which acts as a crystal to generate a clock signal. By using these crystal, we can generate the clock signals and by these clock signals, we can use this clock signals for input sources. PC6 pin are the one where it can be used for the reset option. Resetting the program can be done by using this PC6 pin.

The table below gives a description for each of the pins, along with their function.

Pin Number	Description	Function
1	PC6	Reset
2	PD0	Digital Pin (RX)
3	PD1	Digital Pin (TX)
4	PD2	Digital Pin
5	PD3	Digital Pin (PWM)
6	PD4	Digital Pin
7	Vcc	Positive Voltage (Power)
8	GND	Ground
9	XTAL 1	Crystal Oscillator
10	XTAL 2	Crystal Oscillator
11	PD5	Digital Pin (PWM)
12	PD6	Digital Pin (PWM)
13	PD7	Digital Pin
14	PB0	Digital Pin
15	PB1	Digital Pin (PWM)
16	PB2	Digital Pin (PWM)
17	PB3	Digital Pin (PWM)
18	PB4	Digital Pin
19	PB5	Digital Pin
20	AVCC	Positive voltage for ADC (power)
21	AREF	Reference Voltage
22	GND	Ground
23	PC0	Analog Input
24	PC1	Analog Input
25	PC2	Analog Input
26	PC3	Analog Input
27	PC4	Analog Input
28	PC5	Analog Input

Features:

- *High Performance, Low Power Design*
- *8-Bit Microcontroller Atmel® AVR® advanced RISC architecture*
  - *131 Instructions most of which are executed in a single clock cycle*
  - *Up to 20 MIPS throughput at 20 MHz*

  - *32 x 8 working registers*
  - *2 cycle multiplier*
- *Memory Includes*
  - *32KB of of programmable FLAS*
  - *1KB of EEPROM*
  - *2KB SRAM*
  - *10,000 Write and Erase Cycles for Flash and 100,000 for EEPROM*
  - *Data retention for 20 years at 85°C and 100 years at 25°C*
  - *Optional boot loader with lock bits*
    - *In System Programming (ISP) by via boot loader*
    - *True Read-While-Write operation*
  - *Programming lock available for software security*
- *Features Include*
  - *2 x 8-bit Timers/Counters each with independent prescaler and compare modes*
  - *A single 16-bit Timer/Counter with an independent prescaler, compare and capture modes*
  - *Real time counter with independent oscillator*
  - *10 bit, 6 channel analog to digital Converter*
  - *6 pulse width modulation channels*
  - *Internal temperature sensor*
  - *Serial USART (Programmable)*
  - *Master/Slave SPI Serial Interface – (Philips I2C compatible)*
  - *Programmable watchdog timer with independent internal oscillator*
  - *Internal analog comparator*
  - *Interrupt and wake up on pin change*
- *Additional Features*
  - *Internal calibrated oscillator*

    - *Power on reset and programmable brown out detection*
    - *External and internal interrupts*
    - *6 sleep modes including idle, ADC noise reduction, power save, power down, standby, and extended standby*
- *I/O and Package*
    - *23 programmable I/O lines*
    - *28 pin PDIP package*
- *Operating voltage: o 1.8 – 5.5V*
- *Operating temperature range: o -40°C to 85°C*
- *Speed Grades: 0-4 MHz at 1.8-5.5V o 0-10 MHz at 2.7-5.5V o 0-20 MHz at 4.5-5.5V*
- *Low power consumption mode at 1.8V, 1 MHz and 25°C: o Active Mode: 0.3 mA*
    - *Power-down Mode: 0.1 μA*
    - *Power-save Mode: 0.8 μA (Including 32 kHz RTC)* ***APPLICATIONS:***
- *DIY project prototyping.*
- *Developing varied varieties of projects that require a code based control.*
- *Automation System development.*
- *Learning AVR programming.*
- *Entry level circuit designing.*

CHAPTER EIGHT

MAX 232

Circuit Diagram – MAX 232

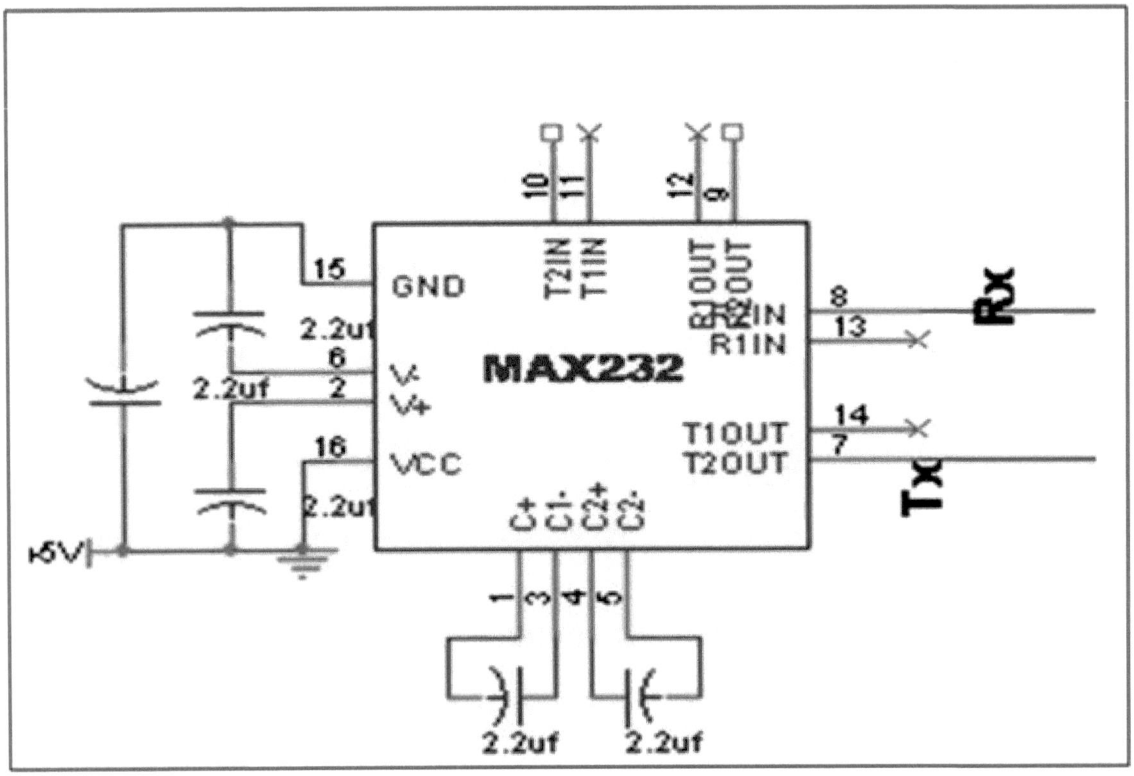

1.It used for interfacing with PC
2.It is serial port
3.It is used to convert TTL signal to RS232 level
4.Typical voltage 1.5V,hysteresis voltage 0.5V
Pin Diagram – MAX 232

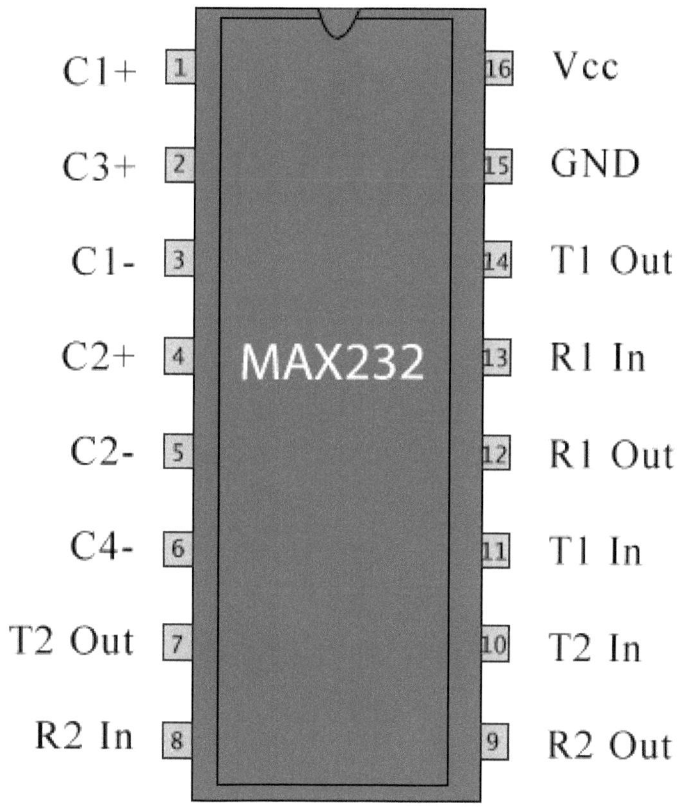

The MAX232 IC is used to convert the TTL/CMOS logic levels to RS232 logic levels during serial communication of microcontrollers with PC. The controller operates at TTL logic level (0-5V) whereas the serial communication in PC works on RS232 standards (-25 V to + 25V). This makes it difficult to establish a direct link between them to communicate with each other.

The intermediate link is provided through MAX232. It is a dual driver/receiver that includes a capacitive voltage generator to supply RS232 voltage levels from a single 5V supply. Each receiver converts RS232 inputs to 5V TTL/CMOS levels. These receivers (R1 & R2) can accept ±30V inputs. The drivers (T1 & T2), also called transmitters, convert the TTL/CMOS input level into RS232 level.

The transmitters take input from controller's serial transmission pin and send the output to RS232's receiver. The receivers, on the other hand,

take input from transmission pin of RS232 serial port and give serial output to microcontroller's receiver pin. MAX232 needs four external whose value ranges from 1μF to 22μF.

Microcontroller	*MAX232*		*RS232*
Tx	$T_{1/2}$ *In*	$T_{1/2}$ *Out*	*Rx*
Rx	$R_{1/2}$ *Out*	$R_{1/2}$ *In*	*Tx*

CHAPTER NINE

BLUETOOTH HC05

BLUETOOTH HC05

HC-05 module is an easy to use Bluetooth SPP (Serial Port Protocol) module, designed for transparent wireless serial connection setup.

Serial port Bluetooth module is fully qualified Bluetooth V2.0+EDR (Enhanced Data Rate) 3Mbps Modulation with complete 2.4GHz radio transceiver and baseband. It uses CSR Bluecore 04-External single chip Bluetooth system with CMOS technology and with AFH (Adaptive Frequency Hopping Feature). It has the footprint as small as 12.7mmx27mm. Hope it will simplify your overall design/development cycle.

It is a class-2 Bluetooth module with Serial Port Profile, which can configure as either Master or slave. a Drop-in replacement for wired serial connections, transparent usage. You can use it simply for a serial port replacement to establish connection between MCU, PC to your embedded project and etc.

HC-05 Specification:

- *Bluetooth protocal: Bluetooth Specification v2.0+EDR*

- *Frequency: 2.4GHz ISM band*
- *Modulation: GFSK(Gaussian Frequency Shift Keying)*
- *Emission power: ≤4dBm, Class 2*
- *Sensitivity: ≤-84dBm at 0.1% BER*
- *Speed: Asynchronous: 2.1Mbps(Max) / 160 kbps, Synchronous: 1Mbps/1Mbps*
- *Security: Authentication and encryption*
- *Profiles: Bluetooth serial port*
- *Power supply: +3.3VDC 50mA*
- *Working temperature: -20 ~ +75Centigrade*
- *Dimension: 26.9mm x 13mm x 2.2 mm*

Software features:

- *Default Baud rate: 38400, Data bits:8, Stop bit:1,Parity:No parity, Data control: has.*
- *Supported baud rate: 9600,19200,38400,57600,115200,230400,460800.*
- *Given a rising pulse in PIO0, device will be disconnected.*
- *Status instruction port PIO1: low-disconnected, high-connected;*

- *PIO10 and PIO11 can be connected to red and blue led separately. When master and slave are paired, red and blue led blinks 1time/2s in interval, while disconnected only blue led blinks 2times/s.*

- *Auto-connect to the last device on power as default.*
- *Permit pairing device to connect as default.*
- *Auto-pairing PINCODE:"0000" as default*
- *Auto-reconnect in 30 min when disconnected as a result of beyond the range of connection.*

Application:

- *Computer and peripheral devices*
- *GPS receiver*
- *Industrial control*
- *MCU projects*

CHAPTER TEN

LCD – Liquid Crystal Display

Liquid Crystal Displays (LCDs) have materials, which combine the properties of both liquid and crystals. Rather than having a melting point, they have a temperature range within which the molecules are almost as mobile as they would be in a liquid, but are grouped together in an ordered form similar to a crystal. An LCD consists of two glass panels, with the liquid crystal material sand witched in between them. The inner surface of the glass plates are coated with transparent electrodes which define the character, symbols or patterns to be displayed polymeric layers are present in between the electrodes and the liquid crystal, which makes the liquid crystal molecules to maintain a defined orientation angle. One each polarizer are pasted outside the two glass panels. This polarizer would rotate the light rays passing through them to a definite angle, in a particular direction. When the LCD is in the off state, light rays are rotated by the two polarizer and the liquid crystal, such that the light rays come out of the LCD without any orientation, and hence the LCD appears transparent. When sufficient voltage is applied to the electrodes, the liquid crystal molecules would be aligned in a specific direction. The light rays passing through the LCD would be rotated by the polarizer, which would result in activating / highlighting the desired characters.

The LCDs are lightweight with only a few millimeters thickness. Since the LCD's consume power, they are compatible with low power electronic circuits, and can be powered for long durations. The LCD does don't generate light and so light is needed to read the display. By using backlighting, reading is possible in the dark. The LCD's have long life and a wide operating temperature range. Changing the display size of the layout size is relatively simple which makes the LCD's more customers friendly. The LCD's used exclusively in watches, calculators and measuring instruments are the simple seven-segment displays, having a limited amount of numeric data. The recent advances in technology have resulted in better legibility, more information displaying capability and a wider temperature range. These have resulted in the LCDs being extensively used in telecommunications and entertainment electronics. The LCDs have even started replacing the cathode ray tubes (CRTs) used for the display of text and graphics, and also in small TV applications.

LCD display use of our project title message and information message. Our project connect to a microcontroller unit data line connected to a 'PORT 2' and control lines connected to a P3.5,P3.6,P3.7.

Pin Description:

Pin No	Function	Name
1	Ground (0V)	Ground
2	Supply voltage, 5V (4.7V – 5.3V)	Vcc
3	Contrast adjustment; through a variable resistor	V_{EE}
4	Selects command register when low; and data register when high	Register Select
5	Low to write to the register; High to read from the register	Read/write
6	Sends data to data pins when a high to low pulse is given	Enable
7	8-bit data pins	DB0
8		DB1
9		DB2
10		DB3
11		DB4
12		DB5
13		DB6
14		DB7
15	Backlight V_{CC} (5V)	Led+
16	Backlight Ground (0V)	Led-

Features:

- *Operating Voltage is 4.7V to 5.3V*
- *Current consumption is 1mA without backlight*
- *Alphanumeric LCD display module, meaning can display alphabets and numbers*
- *Consists of two rows and each row can print 16 characters.*
- *Each character is build by a 5×8 pixel box*
- *Can work on both 8-bit and 4-bit mode*
- *It can also display any custom generated characters*
- *Available in Green and Blue Backlight*

CHAPTER ELEVEN

Android (operating system)

Android

Android 6.0 home screen

***Android** is a mobile operating system (OS) currently developed by Google, based on the Linux kernel and designed primarily for touchscreen mobile devices such as smartphones and tablets. Android's user interfaceis mainly based on direct manipulation, using touch gestures that loosely correspond to real-world actions, such as swiping, tapping and pinching, to manipulate on-screen objects, along with a virtual keyboard for text input. In addition to touchscreen devices, Google has further developed Android TV for televisions, Android Auto for cars, and Android Wear for wrist watches, each with* *a specialized user interface. Variants of Android are also used on notebooks, game consoles, digital cameras, and other electronics.*

Android has the largest installed base of all operating systems of any kind. Android has been the best selling OS on tablets since 2013, and on smartphones it is dominant by any metric.

Initially developed by Android, Inc., which Google bought in 2005, Android was unveiled in 2007, along with the founding of the Open Handset Alliance – a consortium of hardware, software, and telecommunication companies devoted to advancing open standards for mobile devices. As of July 2013, the Google Play store has had over one million Android applications ("apps") published, and over 50 billion applications downloaded. An April–May 2013 survey of mobile application developers found that 71% of developers create applications for Android, and a 2015 survey found that 40% of full-time professional

developers see Android as their priority target platform, which is comparable to Apple's iOS on 37% with both platforms far above others.[17] At Google I/O 2014, the company revealed that there were over one billion active monthly Android users, up from 538 million in June 2013.

Android's source code is released by Google under open source licenses, although most Android devices ultimately ship with a combination of open source and proprietary software, including proprietary software required for accessing Google services. Android is popular with technology companies that require a ready-made, low-cost and customizable operating system for high-tech devices.[19] Its open nature has encouraged a large community of developers and enthusiasts to use the open-source code as a foundation for community- driven projects, which add new features for advanced users or bring Android to devices originally shipped with other operating systems. At the same time, as Android has no centralised update system most Android devices fail to receive security updates: research in 2015 concluded that almost 90% of Android phones in use had known but unpatched security vulnerabilities due to lack of updates and support.[21][22] The success of Android has made it a target for patent litigation as part of the so-called "smartphone wars" between technology companies.

Features:

Interface

Android's default user interface is mainly based on direct manipulation, using touch inputs that loosely correspond to real-world actions, like swiping, tapping, pinching, and reverse pinching to manipulate on-screen objects, along with a virtual keyboard. Game

controllers and full-size physical keyboards are supported via Bluetooth or USB. The response to user input is designed to be immediate and provides a fluid touch interface, often using the vibration capabilities of the device to provide haptic feedback to the user. Internal hardware, such as accelerometers, gyroscopes and proximity sensors are used by some applications to respond to additional user actions, for example adjusting the screen from portrait to landscape depending on how the device is oriented, or allowing the user to steer a vehicle in a racing game by rotating the device, simulating control of a steering wheel.

Android devices boot to the homescreen, the primary navigation and information "hub" on Android devices that is analogous to the desktop found on personal computers. (Android also runs on regular personal computers, as described below). Android homescreens are typically made up of app icons and widgets; app icons launch the associated app, whereas widgets display live, auto-updating content, such as the weather forecast, the user's email inbox, or a news ticker directly on the homescreen. A homescreen may be made up of several pages, between which the user can swipe back and forth, though Android's homescreen interface is heavily customisable, allowing users to adjust the look and feel of the devices to their tastes.[54] Third-party apps available on Google Play and other app stores can extensively re- theme the homescreen, and even mimic the look of other operating systems, such as Windows Phone. Most manufacturers, and somewireless carriers, customise the look and feel of their Android devices to differentiate themselves from their competitors. Applications that handle interactions with the homescreen are called "launchers" because they, among other purposes, launch the applications installed on a device.

Along the top of the screen is a status bar, showing information about the device and its connectivity. This status bar can be "pulled" down to reveal a notification screen where apps display important information or updates, such as a newly received email or SMS text, in a way that does not immediately interrupt or inconvenience the user. Notifications are persistent until read by tapping it, which opens the relevant app, or dismissed by sliding it off the screen. Beginning on

Android 4.1, "expanded notifications" can display expanded details or additional functionality; for instance, a music player can display playback controls, and a "missed call" notification provides buttons for calling back or sending the caller an SMS message.

Android provides the ability to run applications that change the default launcher, and hence the appearance and externally visible behaviour of Android. These appearance changes include a multi-page dock or no dock, and many more changes to fundamental features of the user interface.

Applications:

Applications ("apps"), which extend the functionality of devices, are written using the Android software development kit (SDK) and, often, the Java programming language that has complete access to the Android APIs. Java may be combined with C/C++, together with a choice of non-default runtimes that allow better C++ support; the Go programming language is also supported since its version 1.4, which can also be used exclusively although with a restricted set of Android APIs. The SDK includes a comprehensive set of development tools,[64] including a debugger, software libraries, a

handset emulator based on QEMU, documentation, sample code, and tutorials. Initially, Google's supported integrated development environment (IDE) was Eclipse using the Android Development Tools (ADT) plugin; in December 2014, Google released Android Studio, based on IntelliJ IDEA, as its primary IDE for Android application development. Other development tools are available, including a native development kit (NDK) for applications or extensions in C or C++, Google App Inventor, a visual environment for novice programmers, and various cross platform mobile web applications frameworks. In January 2014, Google unveiled an framework based on Apache Cordovafor porting Chrome HTML 5 web applications to Android, wrapped in a native application shell.

Android has a growing selection of third-party applications, which can be acquired by users by downloading and installing the application's APK (Android application package) file, or by downloading them using an application store program that allows users to install, update, and remove applications from their devices. Google Play Store is the primary application store installed on Android devices that comply with Google's compatibility requirements and license the Google Mobile Services software. Google Play Store allows users to browse, download and update applications published by Google and third-party developers; as of July 2013, there are more than one million applications available for Android in Play Store. As of July 2013, 50 billion applications have been installed. Some carriers offer direct carrier billing for Google Play application purchases, where the cost of the application is added to the user's monthly bill.

Due to the open nature of Android, a number of third-party application marketplaces also exist for Android, either to provide a substitute for devices that are not allowed to ship with Google Play Store, provide applications that cannot be offered on Google Play Store due to policy violations, or for other reasons. Examples of these third-party stores have included the Amazon Appstore, GetJar, and SlideMe. F-Droid, another alternative marketplace, seeks to only provide applications that are distributed under free and open source licenses.

Memory management:

Since Android devices are usually battery-powered, Android is designed to manage processes to keep power consumption at a minimum. When an application is not in use the system suspends its operation so that, while available for immediate use rather than closed, it does not use battery power or CPU resources.

Android manages the applications stored in memory automatically: when memory is low, the system will begin invisibly and automatically closing inactive processes, starting with those that have been inactive for longest. Lifehacker reported in 2011 that third-party task killers were doing more harm than good.

CHAPTER TWELVE

PCB DESIGNING AND FABRICATION

PROCEDURE FOR MAKING THE PCB

1.PREPARING OF LAYOUT

With the diagram and all the components at hand, draw a complete layout plan of the circuit on a sheet of a tracing paper. As a model, for laying the circuit, a thermo Cole base may be used to hold components. Avoid overcrowding of components while making full space utilization. Keep the ground line on the side of the PCB and the supply line on other side as far as possible. When all the components have been mounted on the tracing paper sheet fixed on a piece of thermo Cole base, take out a Sketch Pen for making in such a way that all the connecting wires are equal in width, termination rounded off. Re-draw it on a fresh paper if required.

2. PAINTING OF PCB

The tracing so prepared has to be imposed over the copper printed circuit board keeping in view that the component would be mounted from the non-clad side of the board. Take a PCB lamination sheet and cur a piece of required size of the board by using hacksaw file edges, put the copper clad sheet on the table keeping side on the runway the dirt grease and oxide with a sand paper with its marked side tracing the carbon paper and at her side on top. Since the tracing paper is transformed you can now reproduce a carbon point over a surface but using ball pen on a hard pencil over the drawing on the transparent side. When the carbon print has been obtained over the copper clad board drill ropes in the board using a hand drill. The holes may be draw with 1/32 bit for

componentleadsandthecarbonshouldberaisedorwipedbymistake.Paintth econnecting lines with the help of an ordinary paint. Edges should be scratched with tip of razor blade.

3.DEVELOPMENT OF THE PRINTED CIRCUIT DIAGRAM

After painting the board, it will be made by the cool air for some time. Now take a plastic tray and get some Fe Cl3 chemical powder. The ferric chloride salt is then added with 500ml of water. The color of the solution is pink. Color of the salt is in yellow. Now we add three to five drops of dilute HCL or H2S04. This is necessary to quicken the process.

4.ETCHING OF PCB

Now we take the painted copper clad board and dip it in the solution kept in the tray. After 15 to 25 minutes we see the board, with only printed pattern portion remaining in other places the copper coating is removed due to the chemical action. Then the board is taken out and washes in water. After wash the board by using thinner solution. Now a printed circuit has been formed on the board.

Take fresh water and mix a few teaspoons of Fe CL3 add a few drops of dilute HCL to it, as it speeds the etching process. Shake well immerse the PC Bin the solution for about 20 minutes occasionally altering the solution by giving the seesaw reaction to the disk storing reduces the etching time. Observe the changing color on the copper surface. Take out the PCB only when the un painted portion of the copper surface is completely dissolved in the solution wash the PCB with the water. After the PCB is thoroughly washed remove the paint by soft pieces of the cloth dipped in thinner or turpentine.

5.DRILLING OF HOLES

Then take a drilling machine with 1/32 drill bit to make holes for the incretion of the components use 1/18 drill bit for inset wires and other thick components. Now the PCB is ready to use.

ADVANTAGES:

1. 1. *Reliability in operation and low cost.*

CHAPTER FOURTEEN

CONCLUSION

This project is designed to develop a micro-controlled based scrolling message LED display for notice board successfully.

It can also be used to display latest information anywhere such as colleges, shops, railway stations and other places.

The information is transmitted using an android phone.

Traditionally notice board is all about sticking information, but sticking various notices day-to-day is a difficult process.

A person is required separately to take care of this notice board.

This system displays notices through an android phone on notice boards.

This system reduces the wastage of papers.

9 798886 410747

Printed by Libri Plureos GmbH in Hamburg,
Germany